A Tale of
TWO HOUSES

Written by Melody Carlson

Illustrated by Steve Björkman

Gold 'n' Honey Books
Sisters, Oregon

A TALE OF TWO HOUSES
published by Gold 'n' Honey Books
a division of Multnomah Publishers, Inc.
© 1998 by Multnomah Publishers, Inc.
International Standard Book Number: 1-57673-314-9
Illustrations © 1998 by Steve Björkman
Text by Melody Carlson
Design by D² DesignWorks

Printed in China

For information:
Multnomah Publishers, Inc.
Post Office Box 1720
Sisters, Oregon 97759

Library of Congress Cataloging-in-Publication Data:

Carlson, Melody.
A tale of two houses / by Melody Carlson ; illustrated by Steve Bjorkman.
 p.   cm.
      Summary: Two men build two very different houses in this rhyming story based on Jesus'
parable about building a house on the rock.
      ISBN 1-57673-314-9 (alk. paper)
      [1. Conduct of life—Fiction.   2. House built upon a rock (Parable)—Fiction.   3. Parables.
4. Stories in rhyme.]
Bjorkman, Steve ill.   II. Title.
PZ7.C216637Tal 1998
[E]—dc21
                                                                                          97-45004
                                                                                              CIP
                                                                                               AC

98 99 00 01 02 03 04 05 — 10 9 8 7 6 5 4 3 2 1

To Chris,

May you always build on the

Rock that never moves.

With love,

mc

To Lee, Susan & Andy.

With love,

sb

Both these two men have a job to do,
A house to build, and to live in too.
One will choose to build it right.
But the other will have a horrible fright.
A fright!
That's right!
One will not build it right!

Meet this man, his name is Nick.

He wants a house—he wants it quick!

And so he builds right on the sand.

He says, "No problem, this house will stand."

To stand?

On sand?

Nick does not understand.

Now here's a man, his name is Joe.
Some of you might think he's slow.
Because he wants a perfect spot.
A solid rock, to plot his lot.
A spot
To plot
A fine rock-solid lot.

Well, Nick is fast, Nick is quick.
He builds his house of fancy brick.
His roof is made of finest tile.
And he steps back with a big smile.
He smiles
A while.
But only for a while.

Joe is working—all alone.

It's not easy to build on stone.

He takes his time, he does it right.

Sometimes he works into the night.

That's right!

All night.

But Joe will do it right.

Neighbors come, and it is fun,

To see Nick's house in the bright sun.

Nick paints his trim perky pink.

And when he's done, it makes him blink.

He blinks

At pink

But does not stop to think.

Joe works hard—and carefully.
Sometimes he even works prayerfully.
At last, at last—he's finally done!
He watches his house in the setting sun.
He's done!
He's done!
And now he'll have some fun!

The next day, Nick sees the sky.
He runs inside and says, "Oh my!"
No sooner does he close the door
Than those black clouds begin to pour.
They pour.
And pour.
And then they pour some more.

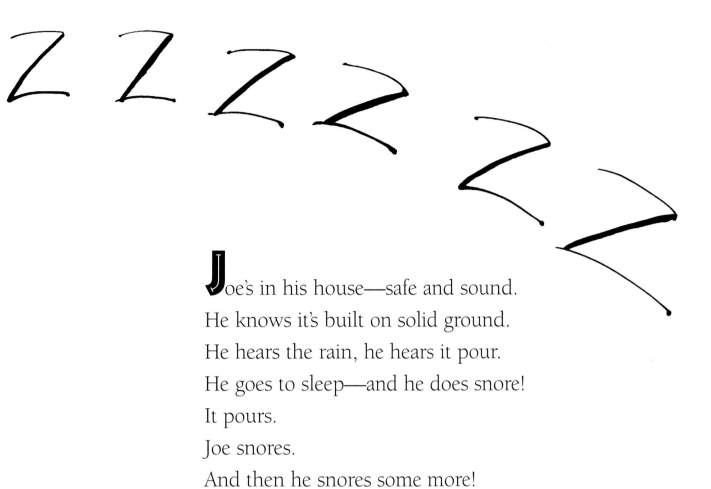

Joe's in his house—safe and sound.
He knows it's built on solid ground.
He hears the rain, he hears it pour.
He goes to sleep—and he does snore!
It pours.
Joe snores.
And then he snores some more!

Nick is worried, Nick feels sick.
Maybe he built his house too quick.
Maybe it's true, a house won't stand
When it's built upon the sand.
Won't stand
On sand
This wasn't what Nick planned.

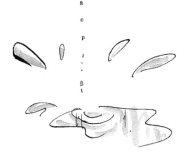

The storm is nasty, it is wild!
Big winds blow, and waves get riled!
Flood waters rise, and start to splash!
Lightning strike! And thunder crash!
Boom bash!
Big crash!
Flood waters make a splash!

Things look bad, Nick sees trouble.
Soon his house will turn to rubble.
He watches as it falls ker-splat!
Tumbling down, until it's flat!
Ker-splat!
It's flat!
It's gone, and that is that!

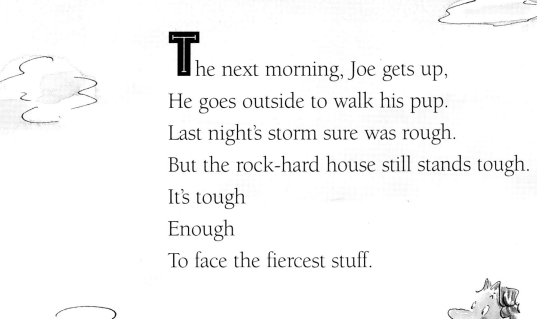

The next morning, Joe gets up,
He goes outside to walk his pup.
Last night's storm sure was rough.
But the rock-hard house still stands tough.
It's tough
Enough
To face the fiercest stuff.

Joe is worried for his friend,
Could this storm have been his end?
He hurries to the sorry sight,
And finds poor Nick in a big fright.
A fright!
A sight!
Thank goodness, Nick's all right!

Nick says to Joe, "I understand.
I see it's foolish to build on sand.
I'll build on rock, just like you do,
A house that's solid and right and true.
I'll do
Like you
On a rock that's solid and true."

Joe helped Nick. It didn't take long,
To find a rock—big and strong.
And if you're smart you'll find One too.
And build your life on the One who's true.
He's true
To you.
And He will see you through.

"Those who listen to my words and do them are like a man who builds a house—he digs down deep and lays a foundation on rock. And when a storm comes and the floodwaters rise, that house will not be shaken. But those who hear my words and don't do them are like the man who builds a house on the sand with no foundation. As soon as the storm and floods come that house will fall down and be completely destroyed."

LUKE 6:47–49 (paraphrase)